The Little Boy from Jamaica

A Canadian History Story

DEVON AND PEARLENE CLUNIS
ILLUSTRATED BY EMILY CAMPBELL

Education is one of the keys to unlocking a child's potential. We dedicate this book to a number of educators who helped unlock the potential in the little boy from Jamaica.

Elwick Elementary school teacher Miss Ruby Hanna, who saw something in the little boy that others failed to see.

St. John's High School teachers/coaches:

    Mr. Bill Wedlake

    Mr. Brian Burdy

    Mr. Dennis Pelisek

Thank you for giving your time, energy, and inner being to help shape many young lives.

Mrs. Joan Lloyd. An educator who gave the little boy an opportunity to give back to her students, passing on what others invested in his life.

Thank you all for changing lives with your generous and caring spirits. May our lives be a fitting tribute to your efforts.

Devon Clunis

Hi there. My name is Devon, and I want to tell you the story of how I became the first black chief of police in Canadian history. I want you to know that you can achieve your dreams and that there are a lot of people who will help you.

I wasn't born in Canada. I was born in a place called Harmony Vale on the island of Jamaica. Do you know where Jamaica is? Jamaica is a tiny island in the Caribbean Sea.

I bet you've never heard of Harmony Vale.

Harmony Vale is a pretty place with lots of green trees, beautiful birds, colourful flowers, and animals, like cows, goats, pigs, donkeys, dogs, chickens, and kitty cats.

There are no dangerous wild animals—like snakes, lions, or tigers—in Harmony Vale.

Would you like to live in Harmony Vale?

My home in Harmony Vale didn't have electricity, so we couldn't turn on the lights. We had to use a lamp to see at night.

Would you like to live in a house without electricity?

My home in Harmony Vale also didn't have indoor plumbing, which means we didn't have a washroom inside our house. We used an outhouse.

Do you know what an outhouse is?

Most people in Harmony Vale didn't have a car. We walked to school every day.

Do you like walking to school?

All the kids wore uniforms to school. I knew everyone in Harmony Vale, and everyone knew me. I was very happy there.

School was different in Winnipeg from what I had known before. Most kids didn't wear uniforms like we did in Harmony Vale.

What kind of clothes do you wear to school?

The schoolwork was very hard for me in Canada. I wasn't happy about that. Do you sometimes find schoolwork hard? Don't give up. Keep on trying. My teacher was Miss Hanna. Miss Hanna was very kind, and she spent a lot of time with me. She told me that I could do it. I believed her.

Do you have a teacher or another adult in your life who tells you that you can do it? Do you believe them? I hope you do.

With Miss Hanna's help, I became a very good student. I love Miss Hanna for helping me with my schoolwork. I also love Miss Hanna for helping me to believe in myself. When I got older, I found Miss Hanna and thanked her for helping me when I was little. She was very happy and so was I.

Even though it was hard at the beginning, I'm glad we moved to Canada. I learned that there were many people like Miss Hanna who wanted to help me. I know that there are a lot of people who want to help you, too.

Do you know who some of those people are?

When I grew up, I decided I wanted to help others the way Miss Hanna had helped me. I thought and thought about how I could help others.

Do you ever think about how you can help others? I hope you do.

One day, I met a police officer who told me that I could become a police officer too and help others. I had never seen a black police officer in our city and never thought I could be one. That police officer helped me and I became one of the first black police officers in our city.

Do you have people who help you to dream of things you never thought of on your own? I hope you do.

I was very happy to become a police officer. My family and friends were very proud of me. I bet that your family and friends are happy and proud when you do good things, too.

I helped a lot of kids as a police officer. I taught them how to stay safe. I taught them how to be school patrol guards and some of them even became police officers when they grew up.

Have you ever had a police officer teach you safety tips? I hope you have.

After many years of helping people, I got promoted.

Do you know what a promotion is?

That meant that I became a leader of other police officers. I got to help them. I did my best to take care of them so that they could go out and take care of kids by teaching them how to stay safe.

I kept getting promoted until, one day, I applied to become the leader of all the police officers in our city. I applied to become the chief of police. That was different because a black person had never, ever been a chief of police in Canada.

My family and friends told me to try my best and I did. An amazing thing happened. I got promoted again and became the first black Chief of Police in Canadian history.

Everyone was very happy.

I learned that, with hard work, help from others, and a belief in yourself, you can achieve your dreams.

I want you to know that you can achieve your dreams, too. Do you believe me? I really hope you do. Because if a little boy from Jamaica can do it, you can, too.

The end.

Suite 300 - 990 Fort St
Victoria, BC, V8V 3K2
Canada

www.friesenpress.com

Copyright © 2017 by Devon and Pearlene Clunis
First Edition — 2017

All rights reserved.

No part of this publication may be reproduced in any form, or by any means, electronic or mechanical, including photocopying, recording, or any information browsing, storage, or retrieval system, without permission in writing from FriesenPress.

ISBN
978-1-4602-9913-5 (Paperback)
978-1-4602-9914-2 (eBook)

1. JUVENILE NONFICTION, SOCIAL ISSUES, EMIGRATION & IMMIGRATION

Distributed to the trade by The Ingram Book Company

Photo by Ginger Johnson

Devon Clunis was raised in Harmony Vale, Jamaica. He immigrated to Canada at the age of eleven. In Winnipeg, the city in which his family settled, Devon endured a significant cultural transition. He experienced the discomforts associated with poverty and marginalization. It was through the care and consideration of invested teachers and coaches that he was able to lift out of his situation and secure for himself the future he dreamed possible.

From the start, Devon had a fierce grasp of his identity as a black immigrant living in a land of opportunity. He decided early in his youth that he would work to set an example for other minority children who were experiencing the same pains of cultural integration, social inequity, and the scarcity of potential exhibited in popular culture. In short order, that took him onto the policing path. The choice was a remarkable one: this was a profession that was not conventionally considered open to people of colour.

Devon was one of Winnipeg's first black police officers. When he was named Chief of Police — the seventeenth in that city's history — he was the first ever black person to assume the post in all of Canada.

Printed in Canada